Introduction to Mennonite Doctrine and Practice

Introduction to Mennonite Doctrine and Practice

by
David Null

Rod and Staff Publishers, Inc.
P. O. Box 3, Hwy. 172
Crockett, Kentucky 41413
Telephone: (606) 522-4348

Copyright 2004
Rod and Staff Publishers, Inc.
Crockett, Kentucky 41413

Printed in U.S.A.

ISBN 0-7399-2316-1

Catalog no. 2356

3 4 5 6 7 — 18 17 16 15 14 13 12 11 10 09

Table of Contents

    Foreword 9
1. Salvation 13
2. The Seven Ordinances 19
3. Public Worship 45
4. Appearance and Dress 49
5. Brotherhood Assistance 53
6. Nonresistance 57
7. Relation to Civil Government 63
8. The Church 68
9. Leaders in the Church 76
10. The Christian Home 82
11. Conclusion 89

Foreword

"Blessed are they that hear the word of God, and keep it" (Luke 11:28).

In many churches today, a number of clear Bible teachings are being neglected. Salvation is often preached, which is good, but instruction on how to live the Christian life is lacking. God's Word gives principles for godly conduct in society, for order in the Christian home, and for the organization, structure, and purity of the church. Every Christian must take Bible directives and put them into daily practice.

This book is designed to acquaint you with the beliefs and practices of conservative Mennonite churches that set them apart from most other Christian churches. Sometimes called "Mennonite doctrines," these distinctive beliefs and practices are based on specific teachings in the Bible, not on the ideas of an individual or on extra-Biblical writings.

In general, Mennonite history traces back to the Anabaptist movement of the Reformation era. Most Mennonites today range from being traditional and not very spiritually-minded to being tolerant, broad-minded, and spiritually careless. However, the conservative Mennonite beliefs and practices referred to in this book are found among those Mennonite people today who understand the value of practical, Biblical Christianity and seek to live accordingly. Though at times labeled as legalists by other professing Christians, or accused of holding to a "works religion," the conservative Mennonite groups realize that emphasis on Christian living does not detract from the redeeming work of Christ, but rather affirms it. They maintain that adhering to Bible principles does not earn their salvation but is a necessary outworking of their salvation.

We begin our journey in the Christian life at the cross of Christ. Regardless of whether we grew up in a Christian or a non-Christian home, and regardless of how good we may have lived, we are unacceptable to God until we trust in the redemptive work of Christ for our salvation. When we are saved by the grace of God, we are also called to no longer live for ourselves but to live for Christ and to submit to Him in all things. "And that he [Christ] died for all, that they which live should not henceforth live unto themselves, but unto him which died for them, and rose again. . . . Therefore if any man be in Christ, he is a new creature: old things are passed away; behold, all things are become new" (2 Corinthians 5:15, 17).

There was a time when I was doing the best I knew to please God. I read my Bible, took part in church activities, and tried to serve God in whatever way I could. Through the example of friends who had become Mennonites, and from reading tracts from conservative Mennonite publishers, I was challenged by several new teachings. As I compared these teachings with the Bible, I found that they agreed, and that I agreed with them. I read about modesty, the Christian woman's head covering, and nonresistance; and I found that these teachings are strong and clear in the Bible.

Until that point in my life, I had not been taught about these things, and I did not know anyone who practiced them. But once I understood that I was not applying these in my life, I could not remain where I was. Merely appreciating the principles and those who lived by them was not an option. I needed to live by the truths that God revealed to me, or I would be disobedient. "Therefore to him that knoweth to do good, and doeth it not, to him it is sin" (James 4:17).

"And hereby we do know that we know him, if we keep his commandments. He that saith, I know him, and keepeth not his commandments, is a liar, and the truth is not in him. But whoso keepeth his word, in him verily is the love of God perfected: hereby know we that we are in him" (1 John 2:3–5).

"For this is the love of God, that we keep his commandments: and his commandments are not grievous" (1 John 5:3).

1. Salvation

"How shall we escape, if we neglect so great salvation?" (Hebrews 2:3).

"For other foundation can no man lay than that is laid, which is Jesus Christ" (1 Corinthians 3:11).

God has provided salvation for all mankind through His merciful plan of redemption. The Christian life is built upon the foundation of faith in the provisions of the shed blood of Jesus Christ and the power of His resurrection. These Bible truths comprise the basic tenets of all conservative Mennonite churches.

Every person is a sinner by birth and by choice.

God told Adam and Eve not to eat the fruit of a certain tree in the Garden of Eden, for if they did so, they would die (Genesis 2:17). The devil, in the form of a serpent, tempted Adam and Eve to disobey God's command, and they yielded. Thus they fell into sin and suffered spiritual death (separation from God). They also brought physical death into the world, which was part of God's curse upon them and all creation.

The sin of Adam and Eve brought the sinful nature upon humanity. "Wherefore, as by one man sin entered into the world, and death by sin; and so death passed upon all men, for that all have sinned" (Romans 5:12). Besides having a sinful nature, every person is condemned because of his own sinful deeds. "All have sinned, and come short of the glory of God" (Romans 3:23). People sin against God whenever they allow something in their lives that is displeasing to Him, whether it be pride, hatred, lying, murder, immorality, unthankfulness, disobedience to parents, or wrong attitudes.

According to the Bible, even those who receive no instruction from the Scriptures understand enough about God to know that they should obey Him. "For the wrath of God is revealed from heaven against all ungodliness and unrighteousness of men, who hold the truth in unrighteousness; because that which may be known of God is manifest in them; for God hath shewed it unto them. For the invisible things of him from the creation of the world are clearly seen, being understood by the things that are made, even his eternal power and Godhead; so that they are without excuse" (Romans 1:18–20).

Eternal punishment after death is the final consequence of sin. Every person will stand before God someday. "So then every one of us shall give account of himself to God" (Romans 14:12). Those found righteous will live forever in heaven with God. "Come, ye blessed of my Father, inherit the kingdom prepared for you from the foundation of the world" (Matthew 25:34). Those found unrighteous will suffer eternal punishment in hell. "Depart from me, ye cursed, into everlasting fire, prepared for the devil and his angels" (Matthew 25:41).

Though Christ called the people of His day to repentance, He accepted young children freely as they were. "Suffer little children, and forbid them not, to come unto me: for of such is the kingdom of heaven" (Matthew 19:14). Children are born with a fallen, sinful nature, but God does not hold them accountable for their sins until they are old enough to understand their condition.

God has provided a way of salvation through faith in Jesus Christ.

Jesus came in human flesh to this sin-cursed world to be the Saviour of all mankind. He was born without sin and never committed sin, as all other men have. Jesus allowed men to crucify Him, He rose from the dead by the power of God, and later He ascended into heaven. This is the Gospel, the "good news" for all mankind. By believing in Christ, repenting of sin, trusting in the provisions of His shed blood, and choosing to follow Him, any person can have his sins forgiven and be freed from sin's eternal consequences. "Whosoever believeth in [Christ]" shall be saved (John 3:15, 16).

Salvation comes only by faith in the work of Christ; it cannot be earned by good works, a religious heritage, or special abilities. "Not by works of righteousness which we have done, but according to his mercy he saved us" (Titus 3:5). God desires that all would receive salvation, and he often withholds immediate judgment against evildoers to allow them time to repent. "The Lord . . . is longsuffering to us-ward, not willing that any should perish, but that all should come to repentance" (2 Peter 3:9).

The fruit of salvation is a life of faith and obedience.

No one can *earn* salvation by good works; but after a person receives salvation through faith in Christ, he will do good works in obedience to God. "We are his workmanship, created in Christ Jesus unto good works, which God hath before ordained that we should walk in them" (Ephesians 2:10). "And hereby we do know that we know him, if we keep his commandments" (1 John 2:3).

Jesus said to Nicodemus, "Ye must be born again" (John 3:7). The term *born again* aptly describes the spiritual change that takes place when a person believes in Christ. The change is so great that a Christian is actually a new creature. "Therefore if any man be in Christ, he is a new creature: old things are passed away; behold, all things are become new" (2 Corinthians 5:17).

The "old things" are the sinful practices of the past life, which will be replaced by deeds of righteousness as the believer lives for Christ. "I am crucified with Christ: nevertheless I live; yet not I, but Christ liveth in me: and the life which I now live in the flesh I live by the faith of the son of God, who loved me, and gave himself for me"

(Galatians 2:20). This is what it means to believe in Jesus.

What if a person professes faith in Christ but lives in disobedience to God's Word? Then something is wrong! "He that saith, I know him, and keepeth not his commandments, is a liar, and the truth is not in him" (1 John 2:4). This is a dangerous course to follow. "Behold therefore the goodness and severity of God: on them which fell, severity; but toward thee, goodness, if thou continue in his goodness: otherwise thou also shalt be cut off" (Romans 11:22).

Christians want to do the will of God, and they will seek help from the Bible, the Holy Spirit, and fellow believers. Though Christians make mistakes, they can be forgiven if they truly repent. "If any man sin, we have an advocate with the Father, Jesus Christ the righteous" (1 John 2:1). However, a Christian must never commit a sin that he planned in advance. Something is seriously wrong if that happens.

Believers grow in Christian maturity in a manner similar to physical growth. In 1 John, Christians are addressed as "little children," "young men," and "fathers," referring to their spiritual maturity. Believers should not be content with being little children in Christ, but should grow into young men and fathers in understanding and practice. This comes by studying the Scriptures, praying for understanding, and most of all, by putting into practice what is clear.

Living for God is a life of certainty and assurance as we rest in His promises. We can know for sure that God will allow us to enter heaven. As we trust in Christ for our salvation and live in obedience to the Word of God, we have eternal life. "These things have I written unto you that believe on the name of the Son of God; that ye may know that ye have eternal life" (1 John 5:13).

2. The Seven Ordinances

> "Be ye followers of me, even as I also am of Christ. Now I praise you, brethren, that ye remember me in all things, and keep the ordinances, as I delivered them to you" (1 Corinthians 11:1, 2)

An ordinance is a religious practice that expresses a Biblical principle. Seven Christian ordinances are taught in the New Testament: Baptism, Communion, Feet Washing, the Holy Kiss, Marriage, the Woman's Headship Covering, and Anointing With Oil. Conservative Mennonite churches maintain these ordinances through teaching and preaching as well as through literal practice.

The ordinances are a direct help in maintaining the spiritual principles associated with them. Religious ceremonies can easily become ritualistic and lifeless, but God's design is that every believer uphold the principles and practices He has prescribed. By regularly observing the literal practice of these ordinances, church members are reminded that Bible precepts are to be applied in practical, daily living.

Baptism

"Go ye therefore, and teach all nations, baptizing them in the name of the Father, and of the Son, and of the Holy Ghost" (Matthew 28:19).

The ordinance of Baptism by water has a prominent place in the New Testament. Christ commanded His disciples to baptize those who believed in Him through their teaching. The early church therefore baptized all new converts. On the day of Pentecost, "they that gladly received [the] word were baptized: and the same day there were added unto them about three thousand souls" (Acts 2:41).

Baptism is commonly practiced by many Christian denominations today, but various ideas are associated with it. The traditional position of the Mennonite Church in regard to this God-instituted ordinance is summarized as follows: "Penitent believers are admitted into the visible church by water baptism, even as they are admitted into the invisible church by Holy Ghost baptism. Water baptism should be administered only upon confession of faith and upon evidence of genuine repentance and conversion." (The visible church consists of a local body of believers, and the invisible church is composed of all true saints throughout the ages.)

Both water baptism and Holy Ghost baptism are mentioned in the previous paragraph. This shows that the word *baptism* does not always refer to water baptism. Other examples are Matthew 3:11, which speaks of being baptized with fire, and Luke 12:50, which alludes to Jesus' baptism of suffering. When we read a Bible verse about baptism, we cannot always assume that it means water baptism. Holy Ghost baptism refers to the experience of receiving the Holy Spirit, which is an essential part of the new birth.

Though various churches use various methods of water baptism, conservative Mennonites use pouring as the mode for observing this ordinance. The water symbolizes cleansing from sin (Acts 22:16), and the act of baptism denotes obedience and commitment to Christ. The mode of pouring recognizes the presence and power of the Holy Spirit, who is described three times in the New Testament as being poured out. (See Acts 2:17, 18; 10:45.)

Baptism is an act of faith and obedience for the Christian.

Salvation comes from understanding and trusting in the work of Christ, not from any work or act of our own. Baptism does not save; it is received because of faith in Christ and willingness to obey Him.

"And as they went on their way, they came unto a certain water: and the eunuch said, See, here is water; what doth hinder me to be baptized? And Philip said, If thou believest with all thine heart, thou mayest. And he answered and said, I believe that Jesus Christ is the Son of God. And he commanded the chariot to stand still: and they went down both into the water, both Philip and the eunuch; and he baptized him" (Acts 8:36–38).

"Many of the Corinthians hearing believed, and were baptized" (Acts 18:8).

Baptism acknowledges the work of the indwelling Holy Spirit.

God gives His Holy Spirit to dwell in, cleanse, and guide every true believer. "Now if any man have not the Spirit of Christ, he is none of his. . . . But if the Spirit of him that raised up Jesus from the dead dwell in you, he that raised up Christ from the dead shall also quicken your mortal bodies by His Spirit that dwelleth in you" (Romans 8:9, 11).

"Can any man forbid water, that these should not be baptized, which have received the Holy Ghost as well as we? And he commanded them to be baptized in the name of the Lord" (Acts 10:47, 48).

Baptism involves uniting with the church.

When someone chooses to follow Christ, he enters into a spiritual relationship with Christ and into fellowship with God's people, the visible representatives of Christ. "Then they that gladly received his word were baptized: and the same day there were added unto them about three thousand souls" (Acts 2:41).

Baptism signifies that the Holy Spirit has joined a new believer to the body of Christ, the church. "For by one Spirit are we all baptized into one body" (1 Corinthians 12:13).

Baptism does not cleanse the conscience or remove sin.

First Peter 3:21 describes baptism as "not the putting away of the filth of the flesh, but the answer of a good conscience toward God." Only the blood of Jesus can cleanse the conscience. "How much more shall the blood of Christ, who through the eternal Spirit offered himself without spot to God, purge your conscience from dead works to serve the living God?" (Hebrews 9:14).

Believing in and partaking of Christ is what frees men from their sins, not the act of being baptized. A believer testifies through baptism that Christ has already made him free from sin and its condemnation.

Baptism is not to be administered to infants and young children.

Baptism is an act of obedience for those who deliberately choose to follow Christ. Infants do not have the ability to make such a choice. Neither can young children grasp the implications of following Christ, even though they might desire baptism as a result of someone else's influence. Young children are safe in their innocence (Matthew 19:14), so it is neither necessary nor helpful for them to be baptized.

Actually, baptizing children can be a source of deception or confusion in adult life. It may cause a person to ignore God's call to salvation because he believes that he is already a Christian. Or if he did have some spiritual understanding at his baptism, he may later doubt that he was truly saved at that time and may wonder if he should be baptized again.

Some denominations practice variations of infant baptism, such as sprinkling the infant with water but not considering the ceremony to have any saving merit. Instead, the parents vow to raise the child in the path of godliness. Though not directly promoting false concepts of salvation, this ceremony can also cause confusion because of its use of water.

Among conservative Mennonites, a person who has become a Christian and expresses a desire for baptism must give evidence of salvation by his conduct. The individual receives a period of instruction on points of Christian doctrine, usually in a class with other applicants for baptism. The church also observes the lives of the applicants to see if they are serious in their devotion to Christ and are in harmony with the church.

After the instruction period has been completed and the applicants have proven faithful, a special service is held for their baptism. The following (or similar) questions are asked just before the actual ceremony.

1. Do you believe in one true, eternal, and almighty God, who is the Creator and Preserver of all visible and invisible things?
2. Do you believe in Jesus Christ as the only begotten Son of God, that He is the only Saviour of mankind, that He died upon the cross and gave Himself a ransom for our sins, so that through Him we might have eternal life?

3. Do you believe in the Holy Ghost, who proceeds from the Father and the Son, that He is the Comforter who abides in and sanctifies the hearts of believers and guides them into all truth?
4. Are you truly sorry for all your past sins, and are you willing to renounce Satan, the world, all the works of darkness, and your own carnal will and sinful desires?
5. Do you promise by the grace of God and the aid of His Holy Spirit to submit yourself to Christ and His Word, and faithfully to abide in the same until death?

After the applicants have given affirmative answers, they kneel and the church leaders baptize them by pouring water on their heads. The baptized persons are then officially declared members of Christ's body and are welcomed to membership in the Mennonite Church.

If individuals were baptized in a different church and desire to join the Mennonite Church, their earlier baptism is usually considered valid if it was based on a sincere confession of faith. Such persons are accepted into church membership upon expressing their support for the doctrines and practices of the Mennonite Church and vowing to be faithful to Christ and the church.

Communion

"And [Jesus] said unto them, With desire I have desired to eat this passover with you before I suffer. . . . And he took bread, and gave thanks, and brake it, and gave unto them, saying, This is my *body which is given for you: this do in remembrance of me. Likewise also the cup after supper, saying, This cup is the new testament in my blood, which is shed for you*" (Luke 22:15, 19, 20).

The night before He was crucified, Jesus and His twelve disciples assembled in an upper room to observe the Passover. This Old Testament feast was held in memory of Israel's deliverance from bondage in Egypt. The feast also foreshadowed the work of Christ in providing deliverance from the bondage of sin.

At the end of the Passover observance, Jesus instituted the ordinance now known as Communion, or the Lord's Supper. With the words "This do in remembrance of me," Jesus instructed His disciples to continue observing this ceremony after His departure.

The focus of Communion is Jesus Christ.

The Communion ordinance is simple but rich in symbolism. The broken bread is a symbol of Jesus' body, which was broken to provide salvation for us. The fruit of the vine (grape juice) is a symbol of His blood, which was shed for our sins.

In another Scripture passage, Jesus said, "Verily, verily, I say unto you, Except ye eat the flesh of the Son of man, and drink his blood, ye have no life in you. Whoso eateth my flesh, and drinketh my blood, hath eternal life; and I will raise him up at the last day. For my flesh is meat indeed, and my blood is drink indeed" (John 6:53–55). Some have applied these words to the

Communion emblems, even to the point of teaching that they are transformed into the actual body and blood of Christ. But it is obvious that no physical food can provide spiritual life. The eating and drinking that Jesus mentioned has reference to exercising faith in Him in order to partake of His salvation.

Communion has both a past and a future aspect. "For as often as ye eat this bread, and drink this cup, ye do shew the Lord's death [past] till he come [future]" (1 Corinthians 11:26).

Communion is a symbol of the unity of the church.

"The cup of blessing which we bless, is it not the communion of the blood of Christ? The bread which we break, is it not the communion of the body of Christ? For we being many are one bread, and one body: for we are all partakers of that one bread" (1 Corinthians 10:16, 17).

Many grains of wheat are crushed to make bread, and many grapes are crushed to extract juice. In the Communion emblems, we see only bread and juice; no individual grapes or kernels of wheat stand out. Similarly, the church is made of many members, each losing his individualism in the body of Christ. When these members observe the Lord's Supper, they are communing with God not as individuals but as a united body of brethren and sisters. How beautiful! "There is neither Jew nor Greek, there is neither bond nor free, there is neither male nor female: for ye are all one in Christ Jesus" (Galatians 3:28).

Believers are to examine themselves before Communion.

"But let a man examine himself, and so let him eat of that bread, and drink of that cup" (1 Corinthians 11:28). Believers are to examine themselves before partaking of Communion, to make sure they are living in Christian victory and demonstrating the power of God in their lives. In fact, they should be continually examining their relationship with Christ and correcting any problems they discover. How necessary it is for us to identify and repent of sin now and not take it along to the final Judgment!

"Examine yourselves, whether ye be in the faith; prove your own selves. Know ye not your own selves, how that Jesus Christ is in you, except ye be reprobates?" (2 Corinthians 13:5).

Partaking of Communion unworthily is a serious matter.

"Wherefore whosoever shall eat this bread, and drink this cup of the Lord, unworthily, shall be guilty of the body and blood of the Lord" (1 Corinthians 11:27). If a person partakes of the bread and cup of Communion with sin in his life, he makes a mockery of Christ and His death. This is no light matter, for such a person "eateth and drinketh damnation to himself. . . . For this cause many are weak and sickly among you, and many sleep" (1 Corinthians 11:29, 30).

In conservative Mennonite churches, Communion is usually observed twice each year. Near Communion time, a preparatory service is held in which the members are reminded of the seriousness of Communion and the need to examine themselves. A special opportunity is given for each member to state whether he has peace with God and man, and to express his support for the church and its standards. Only those who have a clear testimony are allowed to participate in the Communion service.

Conservative Mennonites do not practice "open Communion," in which the Communion emblems are offered to anyone who wishes to partake of them. Participation is reserved for only those members who are living in victory and are like-minded in Christ. This is done in an effort to keep both the Communion service and the church pure and holy.

Feet Washing

"[Jesus] riseth from supper, and laid aside his garments; and took a towel, and girded himself. After that he poureth water into a bason, and began to wash the disciples' feet, and to wipe them with the towel wherewith he was girded. . . . So after he had washed their feet, and had taken his garments, and was set down again, he said unto them, Know ye what I have done to you? Ye call me Master and Lord: and ye say well; for so I am. If I then, your Lord and Master, have washed your feet; ye also ought to wash one another's feet. For I have given you an example, that ye should do as I have done to you" (John 13:4, 5, 12–15).

The same night that Jesus instituted Communion, He also instituted the ordinance of Feet Washing. Jesus rose from the Passover meal, bound a towel around Himself, and washed the disciples' feet.

This was something new. In that time and culture, people would often wash their feet upon entering a house (due to dusty conditions and bare or sandaled feet). Priests would wash their hands and feet as a cleansing ritual before serving in the temple. But feet washing had no part in the Passover feast, and it was very unusual to wash feet *after* a meal. Most unusual of all was for a master to wash his servants' or disciples' feet.

There was a significant lesson in this ceremony. That very night the disciples had "a strife among them, which of them should be accounted the greatest" (Luke 22:24). Jesus, their Master and Lord, was greater than any of them, yet He willingly washed their feet! Thus Jesus taught by example that they too should wash one another's feet as a token of lowly service one to another. This lesson is just as important today as it was then.

Jesus' commands to "wash one another's feet" and to "do as I have done to you" apply both to the spiritual principle and to the actual observance of this ordinance. Believers should serve one another in humility and also literally wash one another's feet as a reminder of the principle and an outward expression of their willingness to serve.

Some say that feet washing was merely a cultural example that Jesus used at the time, and that it need not be literally practiced as an ordinance. But Jesus' actions were not the usual practice of His day. The normal practice was to wash feet before supper, not afterward. Peter's strong protest further indicates the uniqueness of the ceremony and Jesus' special purpose for introducing it (John 13:6–10).

In conservative Mennonite churches, feet washing is part of the Communion service. After the Communion ceremony, a minister reads John 13:1–17 publicly and makes appropriate comments. Then the members pair off and wash each other's feet, using basins of water and towels that are provided for the purpose. (Men and women wash in separate places for the sake of modesty.) The two members in each pair wash each other's feet and then greet one another with the Holy Kiss.

Holy Kiss

"Greet one another with an holy kiss" (2 Corinthians 13:12).

Five times the New Testament mentions Christians greeting each other with a kiss. From the context, it is clear that this was not just a cultural greeting, as the handshake is today. Rather, it is an outward act that symbolizes the spiritual relationship between Christians. It is a *kiss of charity* (1 Peter 5:14), representing the love and family relationship within the brotherhood. It is a *holy kiss*, practiced in obedience to God and in a pure manner.

The holy kiss has been practiced by Christians from New Testament times to the present. The apostles and New Testament church practiced it. The "Apostolic Constitutions" (a writing compiled in the A.D. 300s) makes mention of greeting each other during a worship service with the "kiss of the Lord." Charles Wesley (1707–1788), in the hymn "All Praise to Our Redeeming Lord," wrote the following lines: "The kiss of peace to each we give— / A pledge of Christian love."

Today various Christian groups still practice the holy kiss, including members of conservative Mennonite churches. The greeting is normally accompanied with a handshake and the words "God bless you." Men greet men in this way, and women greet women. It is done in a pure and sanitary manner: a brief contact is made with dry, closed lips. When practiced in the fear of God and out of obedience to Him, it is truly a *holy* kiss, far removed from the perversions that are present in the world today. God's Word can always be obeyed in an honorable way.

"Greet ye one another with a kiss of charity. Peace be with you all that are in Christ Jesus. Amen" (1 Peter 5:14).

Marriage

"And the Lord God said, It is not good that the man should be alone; I will make him an help meet for him" (Genesis 2:18).

Practically every culture has a form of marriage, with associated rules and customs. These marriage practices have their roots in an institution established by God Himself. When man fell into sin and lost his perfection, the marriage bond also suffered. Today the depraved ideas of men have defiled the beauty of this holy union. Even among professing Christians, marriage is often patterned after cultural values and reasonings rather than after the principles of Scripture.

Non-Christians also marry, but Christian marriage is considered a Scriptural ordinance because it typifies the beautiful relationship between Christ and His church. "Wives, submit yourselves unto your own husbands, as unto the Lord. For the husband is the head of the wife, even as Christ is the head of the church: and he is the saviour of the body. Therefore as the church is subject unto Christ, so let the wives be to their own husbands in every thing. Husbands, love your wives, even as Christ also loved the church, and gave himself for it. . . . This is a great mystery: but I speak concerning Christ and the church" (Ephesians 5:22–24, 32).

Consider the deep care and concern that Christ has for His bride, and the devotion and submission that the church is to have toward Him. This gives a picture of how husbands should love their wives and how wives should submit to their husbands. Marriage involves the practical outworking of the headship order (1 Corinthians 11:3) in family life.

Marriage is to be between one man and one woman.

"For this cause shall a man leave father and mother, and shall cleave to his wife: and they twain [two] shall be one flesh" (Matthew 19:5). Polygamy, even as practiced in the Old Testament, caused trouble and grief. Anything other than a monogamous union is not part of God's original plan and cannot provide true harmony.

A Christian is to marry only a Christian.

A basic rule for Christian marriage is "only in the Lord" (1 Corinthians 7:39). "Be ye not unequally yoked together with unbelievers: for what fellowship hath righteousness with unrighteousness? and what communion hath light with darkness?" (2 Corinthians 6:14). "Unequally yoked" accurately describes a marriage relationship in which the husband and wife have different spiritual values. If one partner endeavors to serve God and the other does not, disunity is sure to prevail in their home and family.

The Bible gives direction to those who are already married to unbelievers. In 1 Corinthians 7, the believer is instructed to stay with the unbelieving spouse if possible, but to let him or her go if the spouse wants to leave. The believer must either remain unmarried or be reconciled to the spouse. Peter instructed wives with non-Christian husbands to "be in subjection to your own husbands; that, if any obey not the word, they also may without the word be won by the conversation [conduct] of the wives; while they behold your chaste conversation coupled with fear" (1 Peter 3:1, 2).

Marriage is for life.

Marriage is a permanent bond that can be broken only by death. Even if the marriage "ends" in separation or divorce, the permanent bond still exists in the sight of God. "Whosoever putteth away his wife, and marrieth another, committeth adultery: and whosoever marrieth her that is put away from her husband committeth adultery" (Luke 16:18). "The wife is bound by the law as long as her husband liveth; but if her husband be dead, she is at liberty to be married to whom she will; only in the Lord" (1 Corinthians 7:39).

Adultery is often considered as simply an act (which can be forgiven), but it is also possible to live in an ongoing state of adultery. "For the woman which hath an husband is bound by the law to her husband so long as he liveth; but if the husband be dead, she is loosed from the law of her husband. So then if, while her husband liveth, she be married to another man, she shall be called an adulteress: but if her husband be dead, she is free from that law; so that she is no adulteress, though she be married to another man" (Romans 7:2, 3). The way out of the state of adultery is to separate from an adulterous marriage or relationship.

Though divorce and remarriage is common today and is tolerated by most churches, the Bible describes it as adultery and sin. A valid marriage vow is binding until the death of one spouse. No distinction is made between unions, whether they involve believers or unbelievers, or whether the divorce occurred before or after the partners became Christians. The New Testament allows no remarriage as long as both partners are living.

Marriage is not for everyone.

A Christian's contentment must come through his relationship with Christ, not from marriage. Those who are single are often able to serve God in ways that others cannot. "He that is unmarried careth for the things that belong to the Lord, how he may please the Lord: but he that is married careth for the things that are of the world, how he may please his wife" (1 Corinthians 7:32, 33).

In Matthew 19:12, Jesus speaks of those "which have made themselves eunuchs for the kingdom of heaven's sake." This could refer to someone who chooses not to marry in order to do the work of the Lord without distraction or to someone who has chosen to remain unmarried or separate from an adulterous relationship out of obedience to Christ.

The occasion will be glorious when Christ and His bride, the church, will be united to live together forever. "Let us be glad and rejoice, and give honour to him: for the marriage of the Lamb is come, and his wife hath made herself ready. And to her was granted that she should be arrayed in fine linen, clean and white: for the fine linen is the righteousness of saints. And he saith unto me, Write, Blessed are they which are called unto the marriage supper of the Lamb" (Revelation 19:7–9).

Woman's Headship Covering

"But I would have you know, that the head of every man is Christ; and the head of the woman is the man; and the head of Christ is God. Every man praying or prophesying, having his head covered, dishonoureth his head. But every woman that prayeth or prophesieth with her head uncovered dishonoureth her head: for that is even all one as if she were shaven. For if the woman be not covered, let her also be shorn: but if it be a shame for a woman to be shorn or shaven, let her be covered. For a man indeed ought not to cover his head, forasmuch as he is the image and glory of God: but the woman is the glory of the man. For the man is not of the woman; but the woman of the man. Neither was the man created for the woman; but the woman for the man. For this cause ought the woman to have power on her head because of the angels. . . . Judge in yourselves: is it comely that a woman pray unto God uncovered? Doth not even nature itself teach you, that, if a man have long hair, it is a shame unto him? But if a woman have long hair, it is a glory to her: for her hair is given her for a covering. But if any man seem to be contentious, we have no such custom, neither the churches of God" (1 Corinthians 11:3–10, 13–16).

In the verses above, God spoke through the apostle Paul to confront the Corinthian church with this question: "Judge in yourselves: is it comely that a woman pray unto God uncovered?" The same question comes to us, and the answer is clearly stated. This passage from 1 Corinthians 11 gives the main teaching about the Christian woman's head covering (or veiling).

The woman's head is to be covered to acknowledge God's order of headship.

This order is taught generally in the Bible and specifically in 1 Corinthians 11. Verse 3 clearly states God's order of headship.

God → Christ → Man → Woman

God the Father and Christ the Son are one, yet they have different roles and positions in the Godhead. God the Father is the head, and Christ the Son is under Him. An understanding of this relationship helps us to understand the relationship between Christ and man and between man and woman. The fact that one person is "under" another does not indicate inferiority; it is simply a matter of the designated head being the leader and the other being the follower.

Ephesians 5:23 states a parallel truth: "For the husband is the head of the wife, even as Christ is the head of the church." God's headship order is not a license for lordship, oppression, or discrimination. Men and women are of equal value to God. Both are accountable to God, and both receive salvation as they receive and obey Christ.

The headship of man over woman is a principle that is to be practiced in Christian homes (Ephesians 5:21–33) and in the church (1 Timothy 2:11–15). Women who wear a head covering acknowledge God's headship order.

The man's head is to be uncovered to acknowledge God's order of headship.

According to 1 Corinthians 11:4, 5, covering or not covering the physical head shows honor or dishonor toward one's spiritual head. If a man covers his head, he dishonors Christ, his spiritual head. This refers to a covering with religious significance such as is the

Jewish yarmulke (skullcap), not to a weather protection such as a hat. Conversely, if a woman does *not* cover her head, she dishonors man, her spiritual head—as well as God, who instituted the ordinance.

Praying and prophesying involve speaking to God and conveying His message to others. These are regular activities for Christians. However, covering or uncovering the head should not be limited to certain religious activities, for the ordinance symbolizes the constant reality of God's headship order.

The woman's covered or uncovered head is observed by the angels.

"For this cause ought the woman to have power on her head because of the angels" (1 Corinthians 11:10). *Power* refers to authority. This verse speaks of the covering on a woman's head, which is a symbol of her submission to the authority over her.

"Because of the angels" has several possible interpretations. The phrase could speak of the angels in heaven, who cover themselves in humility and submission in the presence of God (Isaiah 6:2). It could mean that the angels recognize the covering as a sign of godliness, purity, and submission, and the woman who wears it as worthy of special care. Or it could refer to the fallen angels (demons), to whom the woman's covered head would signify that she is under God's protection. In any case, the fact that the angels take notice is another strong reason to observe this ordinance.

The man's hair is to be cut short, and the woman's hair is to be long (uncut).

"Doth not even nature itself teach you, that, if a man have long hair, it is a shame unto him? But if a woman have long hair, it is a glory to her: for her hair is given her for a covering" (1 Corinthians 11:14, 15). These verses, along with verse 6, clearly teach that men should have short hair and women should have long, uncut hair. Though no specific lengths are given, long hair for men and short hair for women are described as shameful.

The religious covering is not the natural hair.

Many people use the clause "her hair is given her for a covering" (verse 15) to argue that the natural hair is the head covering indicated in 1 Corinthians 11. But see what happens if that logic is applied to verses 6 and 7. "For if the woman be not covered [with hair], let her also be shorn: but if it be a shame for a woman to be shorn or shaven, let her be covered [with hair]. For a man indeed ought not to cover his head [with hair], forasmuch as he is the image and glory of God: but the woman is the glory of the man." Such an interpretation makes no sense! Obviously the woman's religious head covering is not her hair.

Then what is meant by the words "her hair is given her for a covering"? Note the context: "But if a woman have long hair, it is a glory to her: for her hair is given her for *a* covering." The woman's hair is a glory in that it covers the shame of baldness that she would experience if she had no hair. (See verse 6.) This is obviously something different from a covering that can be put on and taken off at will, as indicated in verses 6 and 7. Further evidence of this fact is that the Greek word for "covering" (*peribolaion*) in verse 15 is completely different from the word for "covered" (*katakalupto*) in the phrase "let her be covered."

The woman's head covering was not a mere cultural practice.

First Corinthians 11 gives the following reasons for wearing a head covering. All of them relate to spiritual values, not cultural values.
1. Because of the divine headship order (verse 3).
2. Because of principles established at creation (verse 8, 9).
3. Because of the angels (verse 10).
4. Because all the other churches of God observed it (verse 16).

If wearing the covering was somehow related to the surrounding culture, Paul would surely have said so. But no mention of culture can be found in his discussion of the matter.

The woman's head covering was not only for the Corinthian church.

Note 1 Corinthians 11:16: "But if any man seem to be contentious, we have no such custom, neither the churches of God." Paul was saying that no other churches allowed women to not cover their heads. He did not instruct the Corinthians any differently than he did the other churches. The headship order and its symbols were practiced by all the churches of God in Paul's day, and the same should continue in our day.

There will always be objections and excuses for not obeying God. They are not based on the Bible, but on human reasoning and a twisting of God's words to make them say something different from their clear meaning. If it should ever become popular or fashionable to wear a headship covering, all excuses and objections would quickly disappear.

Women in conservative Mennonite churches arrange their hair in a bun and wear a covering over it. The covering is usually in the shape of a cap and is made of a white mesh fabric. Sizes and styles of coverings vary from one group to another.

"If ye love me, keep my commandments. . . . He that hath my commandments, and keepeth them, he it is that loveth me" (John 14:15, 21).

Anointing With Oil

"Is any sick among you? let him call for the elders of the church; and let them pray over him, anointing him with oil in the name of the Lord: and the prayer of faith shall save the sick, and the Lord shall raise him up; and if he have committed sins, they shall be forgiven him. Confess your faults one to another, and pray one for another, that ye may be healed. The effectual fervent prayer of a righteous man availeth much" (James 5:14–16).

The ordinance of Anointing With Oil is an outward expression of an inner confidence that God can heal the body if He so chooses. Observe several points in relation to this ordinance.

Anointing with oil should be done by ministers of the local church.

God performs miraculous healing through local, ordained church leaders. Some people today claim to have special gifts for carrying on a "healing ministry," but this does not follow the pattern taught in the New Testament.

Healing comes through the prayer of faith.

The oil used in the ordinance has no healing ability but is symbolic of God's power to heal. The sick person and the ministers must have faith that God will hear their prayers and heal the body according to His purposes.

Of course, God does not always heal a person who is anointed with oil. To understand why, we need to consider what constitutes a prayer of faith. It is a prayer in which we acknowledge that God is all-powerful and has the ability to provide healing. However, we also trust in the perfect wisdom of God and submit ourselves to His will. We recognize that whether God heals now, later, or never, it will be what is best.

Continued sickness does not necessarily mean that our prayers have failed or that we did not have enough faith. We must have the full confidence that God always hears our prayers and that all His answers are right.

Healing is associated with confession of sin.

Some sickness is the direct result of sin; and in such a case, the sick one obviously must confess the sin if he expects divine healing. In addition, any other known sins must be confessed so that nothing stands in the way of God's blessing. Therefore, confession of sin is an essential part of an anointing ceremony.

If a member of a conservative Mennonite church desires to be anointed, he informs his local ministers and they plan an anointing service. The ministers and perhaps several family members gather around the bed of the invalid. Then the one in charge (usually the bishop) reads James 5:14–16 and makes appropriate comments. He gives opportunity for the sick one and anyone else in the group to confess any sins that they are aware of. Then the group prays together, and the bishop pours a small amount of oil on the head of the sick person. Numerous people have been miraculously healed as the result of an anointing service.

3. Public Worship

"And they continued stedfastly in the apostles' doctrine and fellowship, and in breaking of bread, and in prayers" (Acts 2:42).

From the ascension of Jesus until the present, Christians have come together for worship. Collective worship is an integral part of the Christian life. It is so important that in times of persecution, Christians have risked their lives (and still do so today) in order to worship with fellow believers.

Acts 2:42 mentions several elements associated with worship.
1. *The apostles' doctrine*—instruction in Christian principles and their application in daily life.
2. *Fellowship*—encouraging each other and endeavoring to meet one another's spiritual and social needs.
3. *Breaking of bread*—mutual sharing and oneness, which includes keeping the ordinances.
4. *Prayer*—adoration, requests, thanksgiving, and intercession.

Another important part of worship is singing.

"Teaching and admonishing one another in psalms and hymns and spiritual songs, singing with grace in your hearts to the Lord" (Colossians 3:16).

Conservative Mennonite churches meet for worship every Sunday morning, the first day of the week. Additional Lord's Day worship services are held on Sunday evenings, and mid-week prayer services are regularly held on Wednesday evenings. The following paragraphs describe a typical Sunday morning worship service, though the actual sequence may vary from one group to another.

Men and women sit separately, on opposite sides of the church auditorium. The service begins when a song leader goes forward and leads the entire congregation in singing several hymns. Then one of the laymen holds a short devotional meditation. He reads a portion of Scripture, makes comments on it, and leads the congregation in prayer.

The Sunday school period follows, with classes for the children (preschool, primary, junior) as well as the older ones (intermediate, youth, adult). These classes are held at various places in the church building. The lesson is usually taught from a Sunday school quarterly and consists of a Bible passage with related explanations and questions. The teacher and the class read the lesson and discuss it together.

After the Sunday school period, everyone returns to the auditorium and the offering is collected. (Some congregations do not collect offerings; they simply have an offering box near the main entrance.) A minister serving as moderator makes announcements relating to meetings or other church activities, and he gives opportunity for other announcements. Next, one of the ministers reads a Scripture passage as an opening meditation and leads the congregation in prayer. Then a sermon is preached by a minister of the local church or by a visiting minister of similar faith and practice.

After the sermon, the moderator or other ministers give testimony to what was preached; that is, they affirm that it was in harmony with the Word of God. If any point was stated incorrectly or unclearly, a clarification may be given. Sometime during the service, others in the audience also have the opportunity to give a testimony or to make a public confession of sin or some other failure. After another hymn, the service concludes with a short prayer and benediction.

All singing is without instrumental accompaniment (a cappella). The New Testament calls church members to encourage each other "in psalms and hymns and spiritual songs, singing and making melody in your heart to the Lord" (Ephesians 5:19). Musical instruments were used in Old Testament worship, but they are conspicuously absent in the New Testament.

Children are present during the entire service. Younger children may not understand everything that the speakers say, but they can observe the attention and respect that is given to the Bible, the Sunday school teachers, and the ministers. This helps them to learn how to be quiet and reverent.

"And let us consider one another to provoke unto love and to good works: not forsaking the assembling of ourselves together, as the manner of some is; but exhorting one another: and so much the more, as ye see the day approaching" (Hebrews 10:24, 25).

4. Appearance and Dress

"I beseech you therefore, brethren, by the mercies of God, that ye present your bodies a living sacrifice, holy, acceptable unto God, which is your reasonable service. And be not conformed to this world: but be ye transformed by the renewing of your mind, that ye may prove what is that good, and acceptable, and perfect, will of God" (Romans 12:1, 2).

"In like manner also, that women adorn themselves in modest apparel, with shamefacedness and sobriety; not with broided hair, or gold, or pearls, or costly array; but (which becometh women professing godliness) with good works" (1 Timothy 2:9, 10).

Modern society places much emphasis on appearance. Fortunes are spent on promoting and buying fashionable clothing, cosmetics, and jewelry. How should Christians relate to this according to the will of God?

Outward appearance should not reflect conformity to the world but transformation by the power of God.

People known as nonconformists simply want to be different from others. Their lives are expressions of pride and independence. The Christian's interest is not simply to be different for its own sake but to submit to God and allow Him to do His transforming work.

Inner transformation touches every facet of a Christian's life, including his appearance and dress. When we choose our clothing and hair style, we should ask ourselves whether or not they represent the interests of the kingdom of God. They either contribute to or detract from our Christian witness.

Inner transformation does not mean that we must dress in styles that were common fifty or one hundred years ago. Rather, it means following Scriptural principles with all our hearts, from the inside of our being to the outside. Christians should appear modest, simple, and separate from the fashions of the world. These are the most visible features of the conservative Mennonite faith.

A Christian's clothing should be simple, modest, and serviceable.

Clothing is to cover our bodies, not to draw attention to ourselves. Along with this, our hair should not be arranged in a fashionable style but in a neat, simple way. God's Word teaches that believers are not to wear gold or jewelry; and because cosmetics are also vanity, they too should be avoided.

Clothing should sufficiently cover our bodies, including not only the skin but also the physical form. Tight-fitting clothes reveal the bodily form and are immodest for that reason. Our appearance must not entice others or tempt them with impure thoughts.

Men's clothing should be distinctly different from women's clothing.

"The woman shall not wear that which pertaineth unto a man, neither shall a man put on a woman's garment: for all that do so are abomination unto the LORD thy God" (Deuteronomy 22:5). This principle of sex distinction is found in the Law of Moses, but it is carried over into the New Testament. One example is in 1 Corinthians 11; the uncovered head and short hair of the man clearly set him apart from the woman, with her covered head and uncut hair. A similar distinction should also be found in the rest of our clothes.

Conservative Mennonite women are expected to wear long dresses in modest colors (avoiding bright colors). The top part of the dress is covered by an additional layer of material, called a cape, to conceal the form of the body

For church services or other formal occasions, men dress in long-sleeved shirts and suit coats without lapels. They wear no ties or jewelry. Work attire is to be in keeping with Bible principles of modesty, serviceability, and separation from worldly fashions.

When Christians dress according to God's standards, society takes notice. Those who dress in plain and simple attire stand out as being distinctly different. Such separateness is not due to pride in appearance but to the vast difference between the standards of a holy God and a sinful world. Modesty and simplicity give witness to a meek and quiet spirit within.

"Ye are the light of the world. A city that is set on an hill cannot be hid. . . . Let your light so shine before men, that they may see your good works, and glorify your Father which is in heaven" (Matthew 5:14, 16).

5. Brotherhood Assistance

"*Bear ye one another's burdens, and so fulfil the law of Christ. . . . As we have therefore opportunity, let us do good unto all men, especially unto them who are of the household of faith*" (Galatians 6:2, 10).

God sometimes works in mysterious ways to provide for the physical needs of His people. In the past, He fed Israel with bread from heaven for forty years (Exodus 16:15, 35), and He nourished a widow with a miraculous supply of meal and oil (1 Kings 17:14). Though God can and still does work in similar ways today, the New Testament gives principles and examples of how Christians should provide for physical needs within the church.

Families are to provide for their own needs as they are able.

"But if any provide not for his own, and specially for those of his own house, he hath denied the faith, and is worse than an infidel" (1 Timothy 5:8). As much as possible, individual believers are to provide for needs within their own families. This includes parents supporting their young children and children taking care of their aging parents.

"If any man or woman that believeth have widows, let them relieve them, and let not the church be charged; that it may relieve them that are widows indeed" (1 Timothy 5:16). This verse confirms the fact that families are to provide for their own widows. If someone is a "widow indeed," with no family members to take care of her, the local congregation is to support her.

The local congregation is to provide for unusual needs among the members.

"Neither was there any among them that lacked: for as many as were possessors of lands or houses sold them, and brought the prices of the things that were sold, and laid them down at the apostles' feet: and distribution was made unto every man according as he had need" (Acts 4:34, 35). This passage speaks of the unusual situation in the early church right after the day of Pentecost. Many of the new believers had come to Jerusalem from a distance, and they apparently stayed there longer than they had planned. These visitors needed food and other provisions, so the brotherhood of believers allowed God to use them as a channel for meeting these physical needs.

In the same way, believers today are to help each other when unusual needs arise within the congregation. Such needs may be due to things like a fire, an accident, or a serious illness. Often when a need arises in the life of one member, God provides an excess to others. If there is no excess, Christian love moves the believers to make sacrifices for each other—even of the things they need themselves.

As every member submits to God and does his part in the church, all needs can usually be met; and the result is a sense of brotherhood in both the giver and the receiver. This beautiful scene is possible as each member labors diligently, "working with his hands the thing which is good, that he may have to give to him that needeth" (Ephesians 4:28).

Other congregations are to help a congregation that has an especially large need.

In Acts we read about a great famine that caused special hardship for congregations in Palestine. "Then the disciples, every man according to his ability, determined to send relief unto the brethren which dwelt in Judaea" (Acts 11:29). This relief came from congregations in Macedonia, Achaia, and other parts of the Roman Empire. (See Romans 15:25, 26.) Here we see the New Testament pattern for cases in which local congregations are not able to meet their own needs.

Physical needs are to be supplied by the family and the church, not by an outside party such as the civil government.

The Bible clearly says that God cares for His people and wants them to place their trust in Him. Jesus taught us to pray, "Give us this day our daily bread" (Matthew 6:11). He said, "Seek ye first the kingdom of God, and his righteousness; and all these things shall be added unto you" (Matthew 6:33). God wants His people to provide for their own physical needs within the family and the church. But society today largely depends on insurance policies and government assistance in time of need.

Trusting God to provide for us brings a peace that no insurance can give. He has the power to allow things or to prevent them, according to His perfect judgment. Rather than being *insured* and confident that "the money will be there if needed," we can be *assured* that we are always under the all-seeing eye of the One who has control of every circumstance. Worry about future dangers is the lot of people outside the promises of God; it is not for God's children.

In conservative Mennonite churches, individual families are responsible to provide for their own regular living costs, including minor expenses such as medical bills. Larger expenses, due to long-term illness, hospitalization, automobile accidents, house fires, and so on, are often met through the assistance of the local congregation. If the expense is unusually large, the local ministry informs other congregations, and they may take love offerings to help meet the need.

6. Nonresistance

"Ye have heard that it hath been said, An eye for an eye, and a tooth for a tooth: but I say unto you, That ye resist not evil: but whosoever shall smite thee on thy right cheek, turn to him the other also. And if any man will sue thee at the law, and take away thy coat, let him have thy cloke also. And whosoever shall compel thee to go a mile, go with him twain. Give to him that asketh thee, and from him that would borrow of thee turn not thou away. Ye have heard that it hath been said, Thou shalt love thy neighbour, and hate thine enemy. But I say unto you, Love your enemies, bless them that curse you, do good to them that hate you, and pray for them which despitefully use you, and persecute you" (Matthew 5:38–44).

"Dearly beloved, avenge not yourselves, but rather give place unto wrath: for it is written, Vengeance is mine; I will repay, saith the Lord. Therefore if thine enemy hunger, feed him; if he thirst, give him drink: for in so doing thou shalt heap coals of fire on his head. Be not overcome of evil, but overcome evil with good" (Romans 12:19–21).

These and similar passages teach how Christians should relate to others, especially to those who wrong them. The doctrine of nonresistance, as it is called, is taken from Jesus' command that the children of God "resist not evil."

The instructions in these passages are clear and specific. Christians are to love their enemies rather than hating them or taking vengeance on them. They are to do good to their enemies, bless them, pray for them, and give them food and drink if they are in need. These responses might be called active nonresistance—responding with active deeds of goodwill, not just passively enduring mistreatment.

Nonresistance is different from pacifism.

Biblical nonresistance is often mistaken for political pacifism, but there are major differences between the two. Pacifists simply want to avoid war and violence in solving disputes. They have world peace and self-preservation as their objectives, and they will use means such as civil disobedience and economic sanctions to gain their ends. By contrast, Biblical nonresistance avoids the use of all force—physical, political, legal, or economic. The Christian's objective is not world peace but personal peace through surrender and obedience to God. Trying to convince everyone to live together in peace is a fruitless effort because of the sinfulness of man.

Jesus Christ Himself is our perfect example of nonresistance. He endured great suffering without retaliation, and we are instructed to do the same. "For even hereunto were ye called: because Christ also suffered for us, leaving us an example, that ye should follow his steps: who did no sin, neither was guile found in his mouth: who, when he was reviled, reviled not again; when he suffered, he threatened not; but committed himself to him that judgeth righteously" (1 Peter 2:21–23). Only those who are submitted to the lordship of Jesus Christ can live a truly nonresistant life.

Nonresistance does not apply to spiritual warfare.

Jesus was very zealous for the Word of God. He strongly opposed doing good things "to be seen of men," and He sharply rebuked the religious leaders of His day for their hypocrisy. He was bold to teach the truth even when it was unpopular.

Christians, like their Lord Jesus, should "resist the devil" (James 4:7) but should not fight against man. They should "put on the whole armour of God" and "wrestle . . . against principalities, against powers, against the rulers of the darkness of this world, against spiritual wickedness in high places" (Ephesians 6:11, 12). Believers are to guard their souls and contend for the faith, but they must not use physical force to defend their flesh, their rights, or their possessions.

Nonresistance is a general pattern of life.

Nonresistance becomes prominent in wartime, but it is also a doctrine for times of peace. Here are a few

applications of nonresistance for everyday life.
1. Not serving in any branch of the armed forces or law enforcement agencies, or holding any position that involves using force against another person.
2. Not using lawsuits or other means to enforce justice if we are wronged or injured.
3. Responding in a loving and respectful way whenever we are spoken against.
4. Avoiding disputes and confrontations. If a problem arises and we are at fault, we must go the second mile to make peace. If others are at fault, we should be quick to forgive and hold no grudges, but pray for any offending person.

This does not mean that Christians must silently accept whatever others do to them. There is a place for kindly pointing out an injustice or for appealing to the civil government for consideration of our religious beliefs. (Consider Paul's example in Acts 24.) But this must always be done without force or coercion of any kind. In all dealings with people, the believer's calling is one of helping them to see the truth and find a right relationship with God.

Nonresistance is primarily a New Testament teaching.

If the Bible teaches nonresistance, why did Old Testament saints such as Joshua, Gideon, and David go to war? The Israelites regularly took up arms against other nations, often under the direct command of God. This was especially true in the conquest of Canaan (Joshua 1–12).

The reason is that in the Old Testament, God established Israel as an earthly nation to be a visible demonstration of His glory. Any earthly nation must have political leaders and armed forces for effective operation and defense against enemies. The nation of Israel was also a natural representation of the spiritual kingdom that God planned for the New Testament age.

Jesus frequently emphasized the *spiritual* nature of the kingdom He came to establish. Several times in the Sermon on the Mount, He spoke the words "It hath been said" and then quoted an Old Testament command such as "Thou shalt not kill." Then He continued with "But I say unto you" and added a spiritual dimension that went beyond the literal Old Testament command. It is not enough to merely refrain from killing another person. Jesus taught that Christians must also avoid hatred and ill will which lead to killing.

Jesus clearly described His spiritual kingdom when He stood before Pilate. He said, "My kingdom is not of this world: if my kingdom were of this world, then would my servants fight, that I should not be delivered to the Jews: but now is my kingdom not from hence" (John 18:36). Christ's kingdom, the church, does not consist of just one ethnic or religious group. It is a body of believers scattered throughout many different earthly nations.

Old Testament warfare does not justify Christians' going to war today. But we can receive inspiration from the faith and courage of saints like Joshua and David. As they fought valiantly for the nation of Israel, so believers must valiantly fight the good fight of faith for the church—not with swords or guns, but by obeying the commands of Christ and applying Bible truths to practical situations.

"Thou therefore, my son, be strong in the grace that is in Christ Jesus. . . . Endure hardness, as a good soldier of Jesus Christ" (2 Timothy 2:1, 3).

7. Relation to Civil Government

"But ye are a chosen generation, a royal priesthood, an holy nation, a peculiar people; that ye should shew forth the praises of him who hath called you out of darkness into his marvellous light" (1 Peter 2:9).

The church is a spiritual kingdom in the midst of earthly kingdoms. Christians are to function within earthly kingdoms in a respectful and honorable manner, being aware of the following truths.

God establishes civil governments and appoints their leaders.

"Let every soul be subject unto the higher powers. For there is no power but of God: the powers that be are ordained of God" (Romans 13:1). "The most High ruleth in the kingdom of men, and giveth it to whomsoever he will" (Daniel 4:25).

God uses earthly governments to fulfill His purposes. In the Old Testament, God chose the Israelites as His special people and established them as a nation. He also established other nations around them, according to His will. Through Moses, God said to Pharaoh, "And in very deed for this cause have I raised thee up, for to shew in thee my power; and that my name may be declared throughout all the earth" (Exodus 9:16).

Of the Babylonians, God said, "For, lo, I raise up the Chaldeans, that bitter and hasty nation, which shall march through the breadth of the land" (Habakkuk 1:6). God's purpose in this case was to punish the people of Judah for their sins.

God is in control of all who gain political power, whether through election, appointment by others, or self-appointment. Even when a government leader rises whose values and beliefs are far from Christian principles, the One who "ruleth in the kingdom of men, and giveth it to whomsoever he will" is still in control.

God's kingdom is superior to earthly kingdoms.

"And in the days of these kings shall the God of heaven set up a kingdom, which shall never be destroyed: and the kingdom shall not be left to other people, but it shall break in pieces and consume all these kingdoms, and it shall stand for ever" (Daniel 2:44).

Earthly kingdoms and empires rise and fall, but the kingdom of God stands forever. The church seems small and insignificant in comparison with mighty nations and empires of the world, but God has His eye on the church. He directs affairs in the kingdoms of men so that His purposes for the church might be realized—with the ultimate goal of glorifying His Name.

Many professing Christians promote being active in politics in order to improve society. But God has not called the church to make political changes. The church is to proclaim the Gospel of Jesus Christ to the lost; and when they become saved, the benefit is infinitely greater than that from any social betterment of unbelievers.

Believers are to pray for earthly rulers and pay taxes to them.

"I exhort therefore, that, first of all, supplications, prayers, intercessions, and giving of thanks, be made for all men; for kings, and for all that are in authority; that we may lead a quiet and peaceable life in all godliness and honesty" (1 Timothy 2:1, 2).

"Render therefore to all their dues: tribute to whom tribute is due; custom to whom custom; fear to whom fear; honour to whom honour" (Romans 13:7).

Believers are to be subject to the governments over them.

"Submit yourselves to every ordinance of man for the Lord's sake: whether it be to the king, as supreme; or unto governors, as unto them that are sent by him for the punishment of evildoers, and for the praise of them that do well" (1 Peter 2:13, 14).

Governments enact laws for the order of society and the well-being of the people. Christians should be diligent to obey these laws, including highway regulations and zoning ordinances.

When an earthly government requires something contrary to God's Word, believers must obey God.

"Then Peter and the other apostles answered and said, We ought to obey God rather than men" (Acts 5:29). If obedience to the state means a compromise of Scriptural principle, believers must choose to disobey the state for conscience' sake. Nevertheless, they must still show respect even though they cannot comply. Defiant attitudes are always out of place.

Civil governments in North America have shown much consideration to Christians by allowing various exemptions for religious convictions, which cannot be said of all earthly nations. For example, North American governments have granted the privilege of affirming the truth rather than swearing oaths (Matthew 5:33–37), and they have made provisions for those who cannot conscientiously bear arms. Let us thank God for these blessings, for many believers have suffered fines, imprisonment, and death for their loyalty to God.

A believer's first loyalty is to God and the church rather than to earthly kingdoms.

Christians must not be caught up in nationalism and patriotism. Their citizenship is in heaven; therefore, they have more in common with Christians of other nations and cultures than with non-Christians of their own town or country.

Conservative Mennonites have a policy of noninvolvement in government and politics. They refrain from voting, holding political office, and serving on juries. They will not swear oaths or serve in any branch of the military. They may appeal for exemption from a law that they cannot obey, but they do it without any threat or other form of coercion to gain their end. Christians are citizens of the heavenly kingdom and are "strangers and pilgrims" in this world (1 Peter 2:11).

"Honour all men. Love the brotherhood. Fear God. Honour the king" (1 Peter 2:17).

8. The Church

> "And [God] hath put all things under [Christ's] feet, and gave him to be the head over all things to the church, which is his body, the fulness of him that filleth all in all" (Ephesians 1:22, 23).

The Christian life involves a special relationship with God that is likened to a family relationship. God is the Father, and Jesus is His only begotten Son. By believing in Jesus, we become sons of God through adoption (John 1:12; Romans 8:14–17). We are then a brother or sister to Jesus Christ as well as to every other Christian. This family of believers constitutes the Christian church. God calls the church to function together under the headship of Jesus Christ, the first-born Son, in such a way that brings glory and honor to Himself.

In a general sense, the church consists of all people around the world who are faithfully following Christ. This does not include everyone who makes a religious profession, but only those who have believed in Christ for salvation and are living in obedience to their knowledge of Bible truths. They are making Bible principles practical in their lives, even while specific applications vary according to culture and background. Though now scattered across the globe and separated by natural and political boundaries, this church will someday be united in heaven. "I beheld, and, lo, a great multitude, which no man could number, of all nations, and kindreds, and people, and tongues, stood before the throne, and before the Lamb, clothed with white robes, and palms in their hands" (Revelation 7:9).

This concept of the global church stands in contrast to the modern ecumenical movement, which emphasizes putting denominational differences aside and uniting all "Christian" churches under a general belief in God. The ecumenical movement stresses *unity* over *obedience,* whereas the global church in a Biblical sense includes all people who "do his commandments" and whose names are "written in the Lamb's book of life."

In a specific sense, the Christian church consists of a local body of believers. Much of the New Testament was written to local churches to address specific problems and needs within them. The church in this local sense is the focus of our present discussion.

It is within the local church that believers work together, receive teaching and encouragement, and give a unified witness of the victorious life in Christ. The idea that a person can be a Christian and belong to the global church of Christ without being a part of a local church is not Biblical. Of course, not belonging to a local church may be the case for a time after someone first becomes a Christian, if he does not have access to a Bible-believing church. Situations such as these are unique and usually temporary, and the sincere believer will earnestly seek fellowship with others of like mind.

The church is not to be merely a social club or an association of friends, but a body of God's holy people accomplishing God's purposes. What are God's purposes for the church?

The church is to instruct the believers and encourage them to faithfulness.

Personal Bible study and prayer are essential to the Christian life, but they are no substitute for the church. Within the church there are leaders and teachers "for the perfecting of the saints, for the work of the ministry, for the edifying of the body of Christ" (Ephesians 4:12). God has so designed the church that the members are interdependent. He has bestowed a gift on each believer, but no individual has them all. It is only as believers work together within the church that all the members can benefit from all the gifts.

"But the manifestation of the Spirit is given to every man to profit withal" (1 Corinthians 12:7). As we read the Bible and pray, God speaks to us through His Spirit, who dwells in every believer. When we hear a sermon or when a fellow believer shares an insight, either in private conversation or in a church discussion, God speaks to us through that individual. Likewise, God will use us to strengthen our fellow believers, often in ways we may not realize.

In some religious circles, there is an emphasis on being

tions, symphony concerts, and even college graduation ceremonies. *395 Piedmont Avenue, 404-658-7159, AtlantaCivicCenter.com*

CALLANWOLDE ARTS CENTER – The Callanwolde Arts Center is a great environment for young and budding talent. The center occupies a renovated Tudor mansion on 12 acres of the original Candler estate which includes gardens and nature trails. Founded in 1971, the center plays host to everything from the children's choir to jazz concerts. There is also a wonderful gallery featuring the work of local artists. *980 Briarcliff Road, 404-872-5338, Callanwolde.org*

Insider Tip: The Christmas tours at Callanwolde are a beautiful holiday tradition!

CENTER FOR PUPPETRY ARTS – A former schoolhouse has been turned into one of the nation's leading puppetry centers, the Center for Puppetry Arts. It's a favorite field trip for Atlanta-area schools, but they offer adult-oriented performances as well. *1404 Spring Street, 404-873-3089, Puppet.org*

Insider Tip: Don't miss the Center's annual Halloween Show, *Something Wicked*. During audience participation, anything can happen (and often does)!

DAD'S GARAGE – "Theater without a net" is the theme at Dad's Garage Theater. It's a casual place where you can sit with friends, order a drink or two, and enjoy award-winning improvisational comedy, original plays, crazy musicals, and even children's theater. It's funny, witty, and sometimes gay. *280 Elizabeth Street, 404-523-3141, DadsGarage.com*

Insider Tip: For the wallet-conscious, Dad's Garage offers free programs, pay-what-you-can performances, and even free improv in the Park. Call or visit their Web site for more information.

FERST CENTER FOR THE ARTS – The Robert Ferst Center for the Arts is located on the Georgia Tech campus. The facility includes a 1,155-seat theater that hosts touring and local music, theatre, dance, and opera troupes. The two art galleries off the lobby are filled with works from students and local and national artists. *349 Ferst Drive (Georgia Tech), 404-894-9600, FerstCenter.org*

THE FOX THEATRE Originally built as a movie palace, the Fox Theatre is a reminder of an era of grandeur. The mosque-like structure—complete with minarets and onion domes—offers an interior space that's even more lavish than its façade. The Moorish-themed theatre was built in 1929 and is on the National Register of Historic Places. During the week, there are history tours of this building (see listing under *Tour*) that was almost demolished to make way for a parking lot. The Fox plays host to myriad performances each week, but their summer movie series is a throwback to the theater's original days. *660 Peachtree Street, 404-817-8700, FoxTheatre.org*

Insider Tip: Check out "The Mighty Mo," a Möller organ that was custom designed for the Fox in 1929. It's also the second largest theatre organ in the nation.

HORIZON THEATRE – An intimate 200-seat theatre in a converted Little Five Points school, Horizon Theatre specializes in Atlanta premieres of contemporary and off-Broadway plays. Each year is the New South Play Festival features performances dedicated in some way to the South. Even if our culture remains a mystery to you, at least you can laugh at our crazy ways! *1083 Austin Avenue, 404-584-7450, HorizonTheatre.com*

LIBBY'S CABARET – Libby's Cabaret is a nationally acclaimed cabaret with live music and musical theater served up dinner-theater style. Pay attention while you're in Atlanta and you'll catch an earful of Libby herself performing the national anthem at a sports game or singing with the girls at her cabaret. *3401 Northside Parkway, 404-869-4748, LibbysCabaret.com*

Insider Tip: Don't miss the flashy collaborative performances of Libby's Cabaret and the Atlanta Gay Men's Chorus. Call ahead to find out when the next one is!

MIDTOWN ART CINEMA – The Midtown Art Cinema is the venue for independent, foreign language, and documentary films. The Atlanta gay and lesbian film festival, "Out on Film" is held here annually, and the theater also screens many gay and lesbian films throughout the year. *931 Monroe Drive, 678-495-1424, LandmarkTheatres.com/Market/Atlanta*

Insider Tip: Check out Après Diem (see listing under *Eat: American-Continental*) next door for great coffee and good eats.

NEIGHBORHOOD PLAYHOUSE – The Neighborhood Playhouse houses a local troupe of actors that was founded in 1980. For nearly 26 years, the Playhouse has strived to provide the best in professional drama and comedy for the communities of Decatur and Atlanta on two stages. The main stage seats 170, and the black-box theatre seats 70. *430 West Trinity Place, 404-373-5311, NPlayhouse.org*

Insider Tip: The theatre is just south of Decatur Square, so you'll find plenty of restaurants within walking distance.

NEW AMERICAN SHAKESPEARE TAVERN – The main focus of the New American Shakespeare Tavern is the passion and poetry of the spoken word. But an evening here is also filled with handmade period costumes, sword fights, and plenty of Irish ales and premium brews. The food is authentic to a British Pub—a good place to eat, drink, and nourish the soul and savor a little adventure. *499 Peachtree Street, 404-874-5299, ShakespeareTavern.com*

PEACHTREE PLAYHOUSE – The Peachtree Playhouse is the sister playhouse to the Ansley Park Playhouse (see listing above). Founded and owned by playwrights John Gibson and Anthony Morris, the theatre opened its doors in 1999 and seats 120. It offers a fresh perspective on Atlanta's growing cultural landscape and was the first theater in Atlanta to stage open-ended runs. *878 Peachtree Street, Suite 3, 404-875-1193, PeachtreePlayhouse.com*

Insider Tip: Try dinner at the Vortex Grill (see listing under *Eat: Hamburger Joints*) next door before a performance!

PUSHPUSH THEATER – Pushing the limits and taking artistic risks is what the PushPush Theater is all about. This group is dedicated to the growth of Atlanta's performing artists in film, theater, and music. It's every artist's dream to explore creativity in a boundless environment, and "led by the Spirit" at the expense of being closely associated with a local church. We see the error of this thinking as we recognize that the Spirit of God speaks to us not only within our hearts but also through fellow believers in the church. If we refuse to be part of the church, we actually limit the Spirit's leading by disregarding one of the main ways in which He speaks to us.

The church is to be involved in evangelism.

The Book of Acts is basically a record of the spread of Christianity. The evangelistic efforts recorded here were not the special mission of one or two men; they were the work of God through the church in spreading the Gospel and establishing new congregations. The apostle Paul, for example, did not initiate his extensive missionary journeys on his own. Rather, he was sent by the church of Antioch under the direction of God and with the approval of the church at Jerusalem.

"Now there were in the church that was at Antioch certain prophets and teachers. . . . As they ministered to the Lord, and fasted, the Holy Ghost said, Separate me Barnabas and Saul for the work whereunto I have called them. And when they had fasted and prayed, and laid their hands on them, they sent them away" (Acts 13:1–3).

"And I [Paul] . . . communicated unto [the apostles at Jerusalem] that gospel which I preach among the Gentiles, . . . lest by any means I should run, or had run, in vain. . . . And when James, Cephas, and John, who seemed to be pillars, perceived the grace that was given unto me, they gave to me and Barnabas the right hands of fellowship; that we should go unto the heathen" (Galatians 2:2, 9, 10).

The church is to be pure and keep itself free from sin.

"That [Christ] might present it to himself a glorious church, not having spot, or wrinkle, or any such thing; but that it should be holy and without blemish" (Ephesians 5:27).

God calls His people to "be . . . holy; for I am holy" (1 Peter 1:16). One of the ways the church helps its members to be holy is by identifying sin when it becomes apparent. This is done with a spirit of love for Christ and the church as well as for the sinning individual. When known sin is allowed to remain, it tends to spread and cause spiritual decline within the whole group. "Know ye not that a little leaven leaveneth the whole lump?" (1 Corinthians 5:6).

The New Testament gives several examples of identifying and dealing with sin in the early church. In Revelation 2 and 3, several congregations were strongly rebuked for allowing sin and error in their midst. James 5:19, 20 speaks of the seriousness of sin and the importance of confronting it. "Brethren, if any of you do err from the truth, and one convert him; let him know, that he which converteth the sinner from the error of his way, shall save a soul from death, and shall hide a multitude of sins."

Identifying and dealing with sin can take various

forms. In many cases, expressing a concern is all that is needed to help an individual see his error. Other cases are much more serious, depending on the sin and the attitude of the erring one. Occasionally, an individual will need to be excommunicated (removed from church membership) to help him see the seriousness of his condition. "But now I have written unto you not to keep company, if any man that is called a brother be a fornicator, or covetous, or an idolater, or a railer, or a drunkard, or an extortioner; with such an one no not to eat. . . . Therefore put away from among yourselves that wicked person" (1 Corinthians 5:11, 13).

A member who continues in sin brings a separation between himself and God, and thus between himself and the people of God. When that member is excommunicated, the church visibly removes him from the church to help him see the spiritual separation he himself has made. The individual may still attend church services and have business dealings with church members; but the spiritual bond is broken, and he is no longer greeted with the holy kiss or allowed to take part in Communion.

The motive in all of this is to maintain the purity of the church and bring the erring individual to repentance and restoration. Paul's letters to the Corinthians give instructions on this, first to excommunicate a sinning member and then to receive him back into the church as a true brother when he repents. "Sufficient to such a man is this punishment, which was inflicted of many. So that contrariwise ye ought rather to forgive him, and comfort him, lest perhaps such a one should be swallowed up with overmuch sorrow. Wherefore I beseech you that ye would confirm your love toward him" (2 Corinthians 2:6–8).

The church is to make practical applications of Biblical principles.

All believers are called to apply Scriptural principles in their lives, but how to do this in a practical way can be a challenge. The church is to help its members in this by providing guidelines. The Bible gives an example of this from the early church, when a question arose about Gentiles (non-Jews) who became Christians. Were they required to keep the religious laws of the Old Testament as the Jewish believers were doing? The apostles and others held a meeting at Jerusalem to discuss the matter, and they came to the following conclusion: "For it seemed good to the Holy Ghost, and to us, to lay upon you no greater burden than these necessary things; that ye abstain from meats offered to idols, and from blood, and from things strangled, and from fornication: from which if ye keep yourselves, ye shall do well" (Acts 15:28, 29).

The "meat" question faced by the early church is no longer relevant in present-day America. But there are other questions of how to apply Biblical principles in our time and culture, on which the church should give direction. What is the best way to express principles of modesty? Should a Christian home allow the influence of television and radio? Is there a place for computers or the Internet in our homes? There are dozens of questions like these.

Conservative Mennonite churches have a set of church standards (also called a statement of practice) that give direction to various matters of application. Church standards are tools to help the members practice Bible doctrine consistently. The Pharisees of Jesus' time also made applications, but Jesus condemned them because they viewed their applications as being on the same level as the Scriptures—or even above the Scriptures (Mark 7:7, 8). We dare not add to God's Word, yet we must make realistic interpretations of how to put its principles to practice.

One example of a Bible principle is the teaching in 1 Timothy 2 and 1 Peter 3 on modest and simple attire for women. An application of this principle in conservative Mennonite churches is the "cape dress." The headship covering (1 Corinthians 11) is another Biblical principle; a church standard may describe its style, color, and size.

Some people tend to use church standards as their chief gauge for measuring spiritual status, but that is not the purpose of standards. Rather, members need to give personal obedience to Christ and appreciate the church standards for their guidance in doing so. Believers are responsible to apply all the principles taught in the New Testament, whether or not the local church gives specific guidelines relating to them.

9. Leaders in the Church

"The elders which are among you I exhort, who am also an elder, and a witness of the sufferings of Christ, and also a partaker of the glory that shall be revealed: feed the flock of God which is among you, taking the oversight thereof, not by constraint, but willingly; not for filthy lucre, but of a ready mind; neither as being lords over God's heritage, but being ensamples to the flock" (1 Peter 5:1–3).

Jesus is the Head of the church, but the church also needs human leaders in order to function well. These leaders are to be distinctly different from worldly leaders. As indicated in the Bible passage above, church leaders are to use their office properly—not to gain wealth or power, but to take good care of the flock and serve as examples to them. Jesus said, "For even the Son of man came not to be ministered unto, but to minister, and to give his life a ransom for many" (Mark 10:45). Christ came not to be served but to serve. Leaders in the Christian church should also have a servant mentality.

The Qualifications

The New Testament gives the qualifications that should be characteristic of church leaders. Many of these qualifications are not solely for ministers but are applicable to all Christians.

The principles of the headship order (1 Corinthians 11:3) have applications in the administration of the church. Although many faithful women love the Lord and serve Him in various ways, the offices of leadership in the church are limited to men. "Let the woman learn in silence with all subjection. But I suffer not a woman to teach, nor to usurp authority over the man, but to be in silence" (1 Timothy 2:11, 12).

Descriptions of good leaders are found in 1 Timothy 3:1–12 and Titus 1:5–9. In summary, a church leader should have the following qualifications.
1. He must be free from improper marriage relationships and have a wife who is a faithful Christian. His home and children should be in order.
2. He must not be new to the faith, but should have an established record of faithfulness.
3. He must not be given to wine or the love of money, nor be argumentative or quick-tempered.
4. He must be patient, given to hospitality, sober, and bold in the faith.

In other words, an ordained leader must exemplify the fruit of the Spirit: love, joy, peace, long-suffering, gentleness, goodness, faith, meekness, and temperance

(Galatians 5:22, 23). His life should demonstrate leadership abilities as well as faithfulness under test.

Church leaders are not required by the Scriptures to enter a seminary or receive other formal training. They are qualified by knowing God and His Word and walking in holiness, not by receiving a theological degree.

The Call

God directly called the prophets in the Old Testament; but in the New Testament, God's call comes through the church. If an individual senses a call to give his life in special service to God, he feels what *every* Christian should experience. All Christians are called to live each day for God, serving Him in all they do (Romans 12:1). The call to the ministry is a specific call to leadership in the church, and the church is to be involved in that selection and appointment.

The New Testament gives several examples of ordinations that serve as patterns for us.

The call of God came at times when additional leaders were needed in the church. More leaders were needed either for service in the local congregation (Acts 6:1–4) or for outreach work (Acts 13:1–4). In the former case, the church needed additional leaders because the number of the disciples multiplied to the point that needs within the church were neglected.

The church called men from the local congregation to meet the needs. "Wherefore, brethren, look ye out among you seven men of honest report, full of the Holy Ghost and wisdom, whom we may appoint over this business" (Acts 6:3). The seven men who were appointed already knew the people in the congregation; hence they were better qualified to serve them than newcomers would have been.

If more qualified men were selected than were needed, the lot was used. "Wherefore of these men which have companied with us all the time that the Lord Jesus went in and out among us . . . must one be ordained to be a witness with us of his resurrection. . . . And they appointed two, Joseph called Barsabas, who was surnamed Justus, and Matthias. And they prayed, and said, Thou, Lord, which knowest the hearts of all men, shew whether of these two thou hast chosen, that he may take part of this ministry and apostleship. . . . And they gave forth their lots; and the lot fell upon Matthias; and he was numbered with the eleven apostles" (Acts 1:21–26).

Conservative Mennonite churches have a plural ministry, usually consisting of a bishop, one or two ministers, and a deacon. The bishop is the general overseer who gives direction to the local congregation and other congregations for which he may be responsible. The ministers have preaching, teaching, and pastoring responsibilities. The deacon's primary duty is to look after physical needs in the congregation, though most deacons also assist in preaching and teaching.

The church leaders do not receive a salary from their churches. Because they are responsible to address spiritual needs even when it is unpopular to do so, depending on the church for financial support would create temptations to compromise principle in order to maintain their position. Therefore, the ministers support themselves by their own occupations. (They do receive assistance for things such as church-related travel expenses, and many churches collect a periodic love offering for their leaders.)

When a conservative Mennonite church needs additional leaders, the ministers and congregation counsel together over a period of time to decide whether an ordination should be planned. If a decision is made to proceed, a tentative date is set and the members are encouraged to devote themselves to prayer for God's guidance in the matter. The ministry gives teaching on the Scriptural qualifications for leadership in the weeks or days before the appointed date.

Then the church leaders plan a nomination service, which the members prepare for by seeking God's guidance regarding whom they should name for the office. Other bishops assist in this service, and at some point they gather in a separate room to receive nominations. Each mature male member goes individually to the room and gives the name of a brother that he believes is Scripturally qualified. Those who receive the required number of nominations (which is decided beforehand, based on the size of the congregation) are said to be "in the lot."

Those in the lot are examined by the bishops and ministers to make sure they are sound in faith and practice. After a satisfactory examination of the nominees, an ordination service is held in which one of them will be chosen by lot (after the pattern in Acts 1:26). If only one brother receives the required number of nominations, the lot is not needed and the ordination service is held to ordain that brother.

An ordination service is attended by the local congregation as well as ministers, church members, relatives, and interested people from other areas. For an ordination by lot, identical songbooks or Bibles are used, one book for each brother in the lot. The officiating bishop asks one of the ministers present to take the books to another room and place a slip of paper inside one book. Then he asks a different minister to retrieve the books and place them on a table before the nominees. After prayer, each brother in the lot selects one book. The officiating bishop opens the books one by one, and the brother whose book contains the slip of paper is recognized as the chosen one. The overseeing bishops then charge him with the responsibilities of his office and ordain him to the ministry.

"I charge thee therefore before God, and the Lord Jesus Christ, who shall judge the quick and the dead at his appearing and his kingdom; preach the word; be instant in season, out of season; reprove, rebuke, exhort with all longsuffering and doctrine. . . . But watch thou in all things, endure afflictions, do the work of an evangelist, make full proof of thy ministry" (2 Timothy 4:1, 2, 5).

10. The Christian Home

> "And these words, which I command thee this day, shall be in thine heart: and thou shalt teach them diligently unto thy children, and shalt talk of them when thou sittest in thine house, and when thou walkest by the way, and when thou liest down, and when thou risest up" (Deuteronomy 6:6, 7).

God instituted the home to meet both the physical and spiritual needs of families. Christian parents should see every area of home life as an opportunity to pass on the faith to their children.

Large numbers of people today claim to have Christian homes or Christian families. But all too often, these homes are no different from those of their non-Christian neighbors. The parents are just as likely to divorce as in any other family, the children will probably not continue in the faith of their parents, and the day-to-day activities are the same as anyone else's. Is this the destined lot of all Christian homes? No. It only shows that a determined effort must be made to make and keep the home Christian.

A home is not necessarily Christian just because one

or both parents are churchgoers. In a truly Christian home, the family members put Bible principles to practice in everyday living. The parents use the Bible as the guide for their home, rather than modern philosophies on marriage roles and child rearing. They raise the children in such a manner that they desire to serve and please God and will readily respond to the Holy Spirit when He calls them to salvation.

A Christian home has an atmosphere of peace. The strained relationships and generation gaps so common in other homes are not present. Family members enjoy doing things together rather than each having his own schedule of activities. Children are enjoyed and cherished rather than being resented as expensive burdens.

The focus in this chapter is on some practical aspects of the Christian home, especially areas distinctive to conservative Mennonites.

Relation to the Church

A solid Christian home needs a strong link to a Christian church. The church gives direction and support to families. Husbands and wives receive guidance for married life from the teaching and example of others, which is especially helpful to those who grew up in non-Christian homes. Young, inexperienced parents benefit greatly from the example and counsel of other parents.

As children see their parents appreciate the church and submit to its guidelines, they will also gain an appreciation for the church and its role in their lives.

The Bible and Family Worship

The Bible has a prominent position in the Christian home. Older family members have times of personal Bible reading and prayer. There is also a regular time of family worship, which includes things such as reading the Bible, praying, singing, and memorizing Scripture passages. This teaches children that worship is a daily practice and not just a Sunday activity. It provides a regular time for discussing Bible principles and draws the family together on a spiritual level.

Influences Within the Home

The Christian home must continually be guarded against evil influences. Although the parents strive to raise their children in a godly way, the devil works through the influences of society to undermine their efforts.

Television and radio have no place in the Christian home. What little good they contain is far outweighed by the bad. Even the religious broadcasts are unsafe because they portray a "Christian" lifestyle far removed from what is taught in the Bible. If singing tapes or CD's are present in the home, they must be of the kind that builds an appreciation for the songs and singing style of the local church.

Computers also present dangers to the Christian home. They should be used as business tools, not for game playing, entertainment, or educational purposes.

Involvement with the Internet should be avoided because its dangers are equal to or greater than those of radio and television. Many conservative Mennonite churches have established specific guidelines in relation to computer usage.

Newspapers and magazines must be scrutinized individually to judge their worth. We tend to think we must keep up with the news, but it is often presented in a way that glamorizes the non-Christian lifestyle.

Reading material in general needs to be evaluated on an individual basis. What is the content? Is sin glorified? Is God honored? Does the book present an example of Christian living to learn from? Does it present the truth in such a way that it is an asset to the home?

Parents need to choose books that glorify God and uphold examples of Christian living for their children. Beneficial literature includes biographies of men and women who were faithful in the service of God and books on nature and God's creation. The books in Christian homes must give recognition to God and His greatness, not to evolutionary teaching or "mother nature."

Parents should endeavor to choose right books and read them first before giving them to children. A book cannot always be judged by its cover, its author, or its publisher.

Education

The education of children is a key concern in the Christian home. Learning reading, writing, and arithmetic is not a separate sphere in itself, but is intertwined with children's moral and spiritual development. When children are learning to read and write, they are reading and writing about *something*. What is the *something*? What is the educator's underlying philosophy as he teaches reading, writing, or any other school subject?

Educating our children should be done for two reasons: so that they can support themselves financially and so that they can be useful in the kingdom of God. Education must not be an end in itself. Knowledge must never be pursued only to earn a degree or certificate, or only to better oneself.

The school curriculum must be chosen carefully. There are many things to read about, but why not read Bible stories and other wholesome literature relating to godly living? While a child is learning to read, he can also be gaining a rudimentary understanding of God. In a history course he should focus not only on nations and leaders, names and dates, but on how the faithful church related to the changing circumstances of different periods in history.

Most of the conservative Mennonite churches operate their own Christian schools. This provides an educational setting where the church and homes work together in teaching the children. The school administrators are chosen from among the church members, and the teachers are Christians who live in conformity with the church guidelines. Sound Christian textbooks are available from several conservative Mennonite publishers, including the publisher of this book.

Courtship

One other aspect of the Christian home is courtship, the time in which a young man and young woman together contemplate marriage and a home of their own. When we understand the seriousness of entering marriage and raising a family, we see that courtship calls for sobriety and carefulness. A Christian considering marriage should first be concerned about his own character and consider whether he is ready for this responsibility. Then he should look for godly character in the potential partner. Is that person at peace with God and the church? Is he or she content in Christ in his or her present state, or does the person think life is incomplete outside of marriage? Is the young man mature enough to take his place as head of the home? Will the young woman be able to fill her role of support and submission?

Conservative Mennonite churches have no interest in the casual, social dating that is common in society. Instead, a couple holds to a sober, reserved concept of Christian courtship from the beginning of their relationship. The purpose of courtship is to discern whether a special friend is truly the person that one should marry.

The relationship must be pure and pleasing to God, with no inappropriate physical contact. All physical intimacies, including holding hands, are reserved for marriage. Parents have an important role in lending guidance and support to young people who are courting.

Christian homes do not just happen; they must be made and then maintained through constant zeal and effort. Many a man has lived an apparently diligent Christian life and made significant contributions to his church, but has lost his family spiritually. Though each child is born with a free will and every youth must make his own moral and spiritual decisions, a truly Christian home will have such an influence that all or most of the children can be expected to follow Christ.

"Train up a child in the way he should go: and when he is old, he will not depart from it" (Proverbs 22:6).

"Choose you this day whom ye will serve; . . . but as for me and my house, we will serve the LORD" (Joshua 24:15).

11. Conclusion

You have read about the beliefs and practices of conservative Mennonites. Now study the Bible and see if these practices are Scripturally sound. If you agree that they are, ask yourself: "Am I applying these truths to my life? Am I living in full obedience to God as taught in the Bible?" Do not think these things are primarily for Mennonites. We are responsible to practice Bible principles because they are *Biblical;* our actions must not depend on whether a certain church or denomination practices them.

It can be a struggle to apply Bible principles to our lives, especially if we do not know anyone else who is doing so. Being part of a Biblical church and having the support and encouragement of like-minded believers is invaluable. If you want to know the location of the nearest conservative Mennonite church or would like a personal contact to talk with, please call or write to the publisher of this book.

"For the grace of God that bringeth salvation hath appeared to all men, teaching us that, denying ungodliness and worldly lusts, we should live soberly, righteously, and godly, in this present world; looking for that blessed hope, and the glorious appearing of the great God and our Saviour Jesus Christ; who gave himself for us, that he might redeem us from all iniquity, and purify unto himself a peculiar people, zealous of good works" (Titus 2:11–14).

God longs to have all men receive salvation and live righteously. He wants not only to *redeem* us but also to *purify* us. He desires not only that we look for "that blessed hope" but also that we be "a peculiar people, zealous of good works." May His yearning be fulfilled in our lives.